A Writer's Journal Workbook

With Drafting Prompts

A Writer's Journal Workbook

With Drafting Prompts

JEMM PUBLISHING

JT HARRIS

WRITER'S JOURNAL WORKBOOK: WITH DRAFTING PROMPTS.

ISBN 978-1-989204-27-6

Published by Jemm Publishing.
www.jtharris.ca

A SIMPLE Foundation

A SIMPLE FOUNDATION

Working Title **Readership Level**

Idea/ premise: an example --> Pirates have kidnapped the princess and the main character needs to save her!

Theme: examples are --> romance and rescue - coming of age story - learning about friendship - etc.
The theme relates to the hero's main problem he or she must overcome.

BRAINSTORMING

OPTIONAL: WRITE A LIST OF IDEAS ABOUT YOUR MAIN CHARACTER(S)

BRAINSTORMING

OPTIONAL: WRITE A LIST OF IDEAS ABOUT YOUR MAIN CHARACTER(S)

BRAINSTORMING

OPTIONAL: WRITE A LIST OF IDEAS ABOUT THE PLOT

BRAINSTORMING

OPTIONAL: WRITE A LIST OF IDEAS ABOUT THE PLOT

BRAINSTORMING

OPTIONAL: WRITE A LIST OF WORLDBUILDING IDEAS

BRAINSTORMING

OPTIONAL: WRITE A LIST OF WORLDBUILDING IDEAS

AND NEVER LET UGLY OR HATEFUL WORDS COME FROM YOUR MOUTH, BUT INSTEAD LET YOUR WORDS BECOME BEAUTIFUL GIFTS THAT ENCOURAGE OTHERS; DO THIS BY SPEAKING WORDS OF GRACE TO HELP THEM.

EPHESIANS 4:29

BLURB
Outline

BLURB OUTLINE

Hook/ tagline - The very first line of the blurb to spark interest

Set the scene - Introduce your main character (their name, possibly their age, and any role/job/title they may have, like, superhero, high school student, average teen, princess, etc.)

BLURB OUTLINE

What are the main character's dreams and desires? What makes them stand out from the others?

Primary conflict - What's the problem they need to solve? What stands in their way? What's the object of everyone's desire?

BLURB OUTLINE

What's at stake? (Save the kingdom, but lose the love of their life) Make sure the stakes are high. What is the one thing that will determine everyone's fate? What are the consequences?

Then there's the "Call to Action" (Not necessary at this point, but eventually when you are selling your book online you'll need a CTA eg. Find out what happens in this rip-roaring adventure today!)

NOTES

NOTES

TRUTH'S SHINING LIGHT GUIDES ME IN MY CHOICES AND DECISIONS; THE REVELATION OF YOUR WORD MAKES MY PATHWAY CLEAR.

PSALM 119:105

CHARACTER *Creation*

CHARACTER CREATION

NAME

BIRTHDATE AND AGE

DISTINCT PHYSICAL FEATURES (EYES, FACE, HAIR, AND BODY FEATURES)

CHARACTER CREATION

INTERNAL STRUGGLE (THEIR THOUGHTS AND IDEAS)

PERSONAL STRUGGLE (WHAT THEY STRUGGLE WITH AROUND THEM - DAILY STRUGGLES)

EXTERNAL STRUGGLE (WHO OR WHAT THEY STRUGGLE WITH IN THE WORLD AROUND THEM)

OTHER CHARACTERISTICS AND NOTES

CHARACTER CREATION

BRIEF BACKGROUND STORY

CHARACTER CREATION

NAME

BIRTHDATE AND AGE

DISTINCT PHYSICAL FEATURES (EYES, FACE, HAIR, AND BODY FEATURES)

CHARACTER CREATION

INTERNAL STRUGGLE (LIE(S) HE OR SHE BELIEVES - THEIR THOUGHTS AND IDEAS)

PERSONAL STRUGGLE (WHAT THEY STRUGGLE WITH AROUND THEM - DAILY STRUGGLES)

EXTERNAL STRUGGLE (WHO OR WHAT THEY STRUGGLE WITH IN THE WORLD AROUND THEM)

OTHER CHARACTERISTICS AND NOTES

CHARACTER CREATION

BRIEF BACKGROUND STORY

CHARACTER CREATION

NAME

BIRTHDATE AND AGE

DISTINCT PHYSICAL FEATURES (EYES, FACE, HAIR, AND BODY FEATURES)

CHARACTER CREATION

INTERNAL STRUGGLE (THEIR THOUGHTS AND IDEAS)

PERSONAL STRUGGLE (WHAT THEY STRUGGLE WITH AROUND THEM - DAILY STRUGGLES)

EXTERNAL STRUGGLE (WHO OR WHAT THEY STRUGGLE WITH IN THE WORLD AROUND THEM)

OTHER CHARACTERISTICS AND NOTES

CHARACTER CREATION

BRIEF BACKGROUND STORY

CHARACTER CREATION

NAME

BIRTHDATE AND AGE

DISTINCT PHYSICAL FEATURES (EYES, FACE, HAIR, AND BODY FEATURES)

CHARACTER CREATION

INTERNAL STRUGGLE (THEIR THOUGHTS AND IDEAS)

PERSONAL STRUGGLE (WHAT THEY STRUGGLE WITH AROUND THEM - DAILY STRUGGLES)

EXTERNAL STRUGGLE (WHO OR WHAT THEY STRUGGLE WITH IN THE WORLD AROUND THEM)

OTHER CHARACTERISTICS AND NOTES

CHARACTER CREATION

BRIEF BACKGROUND STORY

CHARACTER CREATION

NAME

BIRTHDATE AND AGE

DISTINCT PHYSICAL FEATURES (EYES, FACE, HAIR, AND BODY FEATURES)

CHARACTER CREATION

INTERNAL STRUGGLE (THEIR THOUGHTS AND IDEAS)

PERSONAL STRUGGLE (WHAT THEY STRUGGLE WITH AROUND THEM - DAILY STRUGGLES)

EXTERNAL STRUGGLE (WHO OR WHAT THEY STRUGGLE WITH IN THE WORLD AROUND THEM)

OTHER CHARACTERISTICS AND NOTES

CHARACTER CREATION

BRIEF BACKGROUND STORY

DO YOU WANT TO LIVE A LONG,
GOOD LIFE,
ENJOYING THE BEAUTY THAT FILLS
EACH DAY?
THEN NEVER SPEAK A LIE OR ALLOW
WICKED WORDS
TO COME FROM YOUR MOUTH.

PSALM 34:12-13

ROUGH
Outline

OPENING SCENE/ ORDINARY LIFE

CHALLENGING EVENT/ INCITING INCIDENT

ADVENTURE STARTS/ NEW LIFE BEGINS

PROBLEM ARISES/ FUN AND GAMES

COMPLICATIONS/ FUN AND GAMES CONTINUED

NEW PROBLEM REVEALED

SOLVING PROBLEM THE WRONG WAY

NEW COMPLICATIONS

FALSE VICTORY/
FALSE DEFEAT

BAD GUYS CLOSE IN/ A SHIFT

ALL IS LOST

REFLECTING/
REACTING

PROACTIVE DECISION TO CHANGE THE RIGHT WAY

CLIMAX

PROBLEM SOLVED/ BAD GUYS DEFEATED

RESOLVED/ NEW LIFE BEGINS

OPENING SCENE/ ORDINARY LIFE

(ELABORATE/EXPAND)

CHALLENGING EVENT/ INCITING INCIDENT

(ELABORATE/EXPAND)

ADVENTURE STARTS/ NEW LIFE BEGINS

(ELABORATE/EXPAND)

PROBLEM ARISES/ FUN AND GAMES

(ELABORATE/EXPAND)

COMPLICATIONS/ FUN AND GAMES CONTINUED

(ELABORATE/EXPAND)

NEW PROBLEM REVEALED

(ELABORATE/EXPAND)

SOLVING THE PROBLEM THE WRONG WAY

(ELABORATE/EXPAND)

NEW COMPLICATIONS

(ELABORATE/EXPAND)

FALSE VICTORY/ FALSE DEFEAT

(ELABORATE/EXPAND)

BAD GUYS CLOSE IN/ A SHIFT

(ELABORATE/EXPAND)

ALL IS LOST

(ELABORATE/EXPAND)

REFLECTING/ REACTING

(ELABORATE/EXPAND)

PROACTIVE DECISION TO CHANGE THE RIGHT WAY

(ELABORATE/EXPAND)

CLIMAX

(ELABORATE/EXPAND)

PROBLEM SOLVED/ BAD GUYS DEFEATED

(ELABORATE/EXPAND)

RESOLVED/ NEW LIFE BEGINS

(ELABORATE/EXPAND)

NOTHING IS MORE APPEALING THAN SPEAKING BEAUTIFUL, LIFE-GIVING WORDS.
FOR THEY RELEASE SWEETNESS TO OUR SOULS
AND INNER HEALING TO OUR SPIRITS.

PROVERBS 16:24

SCENE
Builder

SCENE BUILDER

POV CHARACTER:

SCENE DESCRIPTIONS

USE FIVE SENSES - SIGHT, SMELL, SOUND, TASTE, TOUCH (TEXTURE)

ROUGH DRAFT
(GOAL OF SCENE)

WHAT IS THE MAIN CHARACTER THINKING AND FEELING DURING THIS SCENE?

ROUGH DRAFT
(PROBLEM OF THE SCENE)

WHAT ARE THE SIDE CHARACTERS THINKING AND FEELING?

ROUGH DRAFT

CHARACTERS TAKE ACTION - WHAT IS THE GOAL?

ROUGH DRAFT

HOW ARE THE CHARACTERS CHALLENGED?

ROUGH DRAFT
(CHOICES/ REVEALING CHARACTER)

HOW DO THE CHARACTERS HANDLE THE CHALLENGE?

ROUGH DRAFT
(CONSEQUENCES/ NEW PROBLEM)

WHAT CHOICES ARE
THEY FORCED TO
MAKE?

NEW SCENE

POV CHARACTER:

SCENE DESCRIPTIONS

USE FIVE SENSES - SIGHT, SMELL, SOUND, TASTE, TOUCH (TEXTURE)

ROUGH DRAFT
(GOAL OF SCENE)

WHAT IS THE MAIN CHARACTER THINKING AND FEELING DURING THIS SCENE?

ROUGH DRAFT
(PROBLEM OF THE SCENE)

WHAT ARE THE SIDE CHARACTERS THINKING AND FEELING?

ROUGH DRAFT

CHARACTERS TAKE ACTION - WHAT IS THE GOAL?

ROUGH DRAFT

HOW ARE THE CHARACTERS CHALLENGED?

ROUGH DRAFT
(CHOICES/ REVEALING CHARACTER)

HOW DO THE
CHARACTERS HANDLE
THE CHALLENGE?

ROUGH DRAFT
(CONSEQUENCES/ NEW PROBLEM)

WHAT CHOICES ARE THEY FORCED TO MAKE?

NEW SCENE

POV CHARACTER:

SCENE DESCRIPTIONS

USE FIVE SENSES - SIGHT, SMELL, SOUND, TASTE, TOUCH (TEXTURE)

ROUGH DRAFT
(GOAL OF SCENE)

WHAT IS THE MAIN CHARACTER THINKING AND FEELING DURING THIS SCENE?

ROUGH DRAFT
(PROBLEM OF THE SCENE)

WHAT ARE THE SIDE CHARACTERS THINKING AND FEELING?

ROUGH DRAFT

CHARACTERS TAKE ACTION - WHAT IS THE GOAL?

ROUGH DRAFT

HOW ARE THE CHARACTERS CHALLENGED?

ROUGH DRAFT
(CHOICES/ REVEALING CHARACTER)

HOW DO THE CHARACTERS HANDLE THE CHALLENGE?

ROUGH DRAFT
(CONSEQUENCES/ NEW PROBLEM)

WHAT CHOICES ARE
THEY FORCED TO
MAKE?

NEW SCENE

POV CHARACTER:

SCENE DESCRIPTIONS

USE FIVE SENSES - SIGHT, SMELL, SOUND, TASTE, TOUCH (TEXTURE)

ROUGH DRAFT
(GOAL OF SCENE)

WHAT IS THE MAIN CHARACTER THINKING AND FEELING DURING THIS SCENE?

ROUGH DRAFT
(PROBLEM OF THE SCENE)

WHAT ARE THE SIDE CHARACTERS THINKING AND FEELING?

ROUGH DRAFT

CHARACTERS TAKE ACTION - WHAT IS THE GOAL?

ROUGH DRAFT

HOW ARE THE CHARACTERS CHALLENGED?

ROUGH DRAFT
(CHOICES/ REVEALING CHARACTER)

HOW DO THE
CHARACTERS HANDLE
THE CHALLENGE?

ROUGH DRAFT
(CONSEQUENCES/ NEW PROBLEM)

WHAT CHOICES ARE THEY FORCED TO MAKE?

NEW SCENE

POV CHARACTER:

SCENE DESCRIPTIONS

USE FIVE SENSES - SIGHT, SMELL, SOUND, TASTE, TOUCH (TEXTURE)

ROUGH DRAFT
(GOAL OF SCENE)

WHAT IS THE MAIN CHARACTER THINKING AND FEELING DURING THIS SCENE?

ROUGH DRAFT
(PROBLEM OF THE SCENE)

WHAT ARE THE SIDE CHARACTERS THINKING AND FEELING?

ROUGH DRAFT

CHARACTERS TAKE ACTION - WHAT IS THE GOAL?

ROUGH DRAFT

HOW ARE THE CHARACTERS CHALLENGED?

ROUGH DRAFT
(CHOICES/ REVEALING CHARACTER)

HOW DO THE CHARACTERS HANDLE THE CHALLENGE?

ROUGH DRAFT
(CONSEQUENCES/ NEW PROBLEM)

WHAT CHOICES ARE THEY FORCED TO MAKE?

NEW SCENE

POV CHARACTER:

SCENE DESCRIPTIONS

USE FIVE SENSES - SIGHT, SMELL, SOUND, TASTE, TOUCH (TEXTURE)

ROUGH DRAFT
(GOAL OF SCENE)

WHAT IS THE MAIN
CHARACTER THINKING
AND FEELING DURING
THIS SCENE?

ROUGH DRAFT
(PROBLEM OF THE SCENE)

WHAT ARE THE SIDE CHARACTERS THINKING AND FEELING?

ROUGH DRAFT

CHARACTERS TAKE ACTION - WHAT IS THE GOAL?

ROUGH DRAFT

HOW ARE THE CHARACTERS CHALLENGED?

ROUGH DRAFT
(CHOICES/ REVEALING CHARACTER)

HOW DO THE
CHARACTERS HANDLE
THE CHALLENGE?

ROUGH DRAFT
(CONSEQUENCES/ NEW PROBLEM)

WHAT CHOICES ARE
THEY FORCED TO
MAKE?

NEW SCENE

POV CHARACTER:

SCENE DESCRIPTIONS

USE FIVE SENSES - SIGHT, SMELL, SOUND, TASTE, TOUCH (TEXTURE)

ROUGH DRAFT
(GOAL OF SCENE)

WHAT IS THE MAIN CHARACTER THINKING AND FEELING DURING THIS SCENE?

ROUGH DRAFT
(PROBLEM OF THE SCENE)

WHAT ARE THE SIDE CHARACTERS THINKING AND FEELING?

ROUGH DRAFT

CHARACTERS TAKE ACTION - WHAT IS THE GOAL?

ROUGH DRAFT

HOW ARE THE CHARACTERS CHALLENGED?

ROUGH DRAFT
(CHOICES/ REVEALING CHARACTER)

HOW DO THE
CHARACTERS HANDLE
THE CHALLENGE?

ROUGH DRAFT
(CONSEQUENCES/ NEW PROBLEM)

WHAT CHOICES ARE THEY FORCED TO MAKE?

NEW SCENE

POV CHARACTER:

SCENE DESCRIPTIONS

USE FIVE SENSES - SIGHT, SMELL, SOUND, TASTE, TOUCH (TEXTURE)

ROUGH DRAFT
(GOAL OF SCENE)

WHAT IS THE MAIN CHARACTER THINKING AND FEELING DURING THIS SCENE?

ROUGH DRAFT
(PROBLEM OF THE SCENE)

WHAT ARE THE SIDE CHARACTERS THINKING AND FEELING?

ROUGH DRAFT

CHARACTERS TAKE ACTION - WHAT IS THE GOAL?

ROUGH DRAFT

HOW ARE THE CHARACTERS CHALLENGED?

ROUGH DRAFT
(CHOICES/ REVEALING CHARACTER)

HOW DO THE CHARACTERS HANDLE THE CHALLENGE?

ROUGH DRAFT
(CONSEQUENCES/ NEW PROBLEM)

WHAT CHOICES ARE THEY FORCED TO MAKE?

NEW SCENE

POV CHARACTER:

SCENE DESCRIPTIONS

USE FIVE SENSES - SIGHT, SMELL, SOUND, TASTE, TOUCH (TEXTURE)

ROUGH DRAFT
(GOAL OF SCENE)

WHAT IS THE MAIN CHARACTER THINKING AND FEELING DURING THIS SCENE?

ROUGH DRAFT
(PROBLEM OF THE SCENE)

WHAT ARE THE SIDE CHARACTERS THINKING AND FEELING?

ROUGH DRAFT

CHARACTERS TAKE ACTION - WHAT IS THE GOAL?

ROUGH DRAFT

HOW ARE THE CHARACTERS CHALLENGED?

ROUGH DRAFT
(CHOICES/ REVEALING CHARACTER)

HOW DO THE CHARACTERS HANDLE THE CHALLENGE?

ROUGH DRAFT
(CONSEQUENCES/ NEW PROBLEM)

WHAT CHOICES ARE
THEY FORCED TO
MAKE?

NEW SCENE

POV CHARACTER:

SCENE DESCRIPTIONS

USE FIVE SENSES - SIGHT, SMELL, SOUND, TASTE, TOUCH (TEXTURE)

ROUGH DRAFT
(GOAL OF SCENE)

WHAT IS THE MAIN CHARACTER THINKING AND FEELING DURING THIS SCENE?

ROUGH DRAFT
(PROBLEM OF THE SCENE)

WHAT ARE THE SIDE CHARACTERS THINKING AND FEELING?

ROUGH DRAFT

CHARACTERS TAKE ACTION - WHAT IS THE GOAL?

ROUGH DRAFT

HOW ARE THE CHARACTERS CHALLENGED?

ROUGH DRAFT
(CHOICES/ REVEALING CHARACTER)

HOW DO THE
CHARACTERS HANDLE
THE CHALLENGE?

ROUGH DRAFT
(CONSEQUENCES/ NEW PROBLEM)

WHAT CHOICES ARE THEY FORCED TO MAKE?

NEW SCENE

POV CHARACTER:

SCENE DESCRIPTIONS

USE FIVE SENSES - SIGHT, SMELL, SOUND, TASTE, TOUCH (TEXTURE)

ROUGH DRAFT
(GOAL OF SCENE)

WHAT IS THE MAIN CHARACTER THINKING AND FEELING DURING THIS SCENE?

ROUGH DRAFT
(PROBLEM OF THE SCENE)

WHAT ARE THE SIDE CHARACTERS THINKING AND FEELING?

ROUGH DRAFT

CHARACTERS TAKE ACTION - WHAT IS THE GOAL?

ROUGH DRAFT

HOW ARE THE CHARACTERS CHALLENGED?

ROUGH DRAFT
(CHOICES/ REVEALING CHARACTER)

HOW DO THE
CHARACTERS HANDLE
THE CHALLENGE?

ROUGH DRAFT
(CONSEQUENCES/ NEW PROBLEM)

WHAT CHOICES ARE THEY FORCED TO MAKE?

NEW SCENE

POV CHARACTER:

SCENE DESCRIPTIONS

USE FIVE SENSES - SIGHT, SMELL, SOUND, TASTE, TOUCH (TEXTURE)

ROUGH DRAFT
(GOAL OF SCENE)

WHAT IS THE MAIN CHARACTER THINKING AND FEELING DURING THIS SCENE?

ROUGH DRAFT
(PROBLEM OF THE SCENE)

WHAT ARE THE SIDE CHARACTERS THINKING AND FEELING?

ROUGH DRAFT

CHARACTERS TAKE ACTION - WHAT IS THE GOAL?

ROUGH DRAFT

HOW ARE THE CHARACTERS CHALLENGED?

ROUGH DRAFT
(CHOICES/ REVEALING CHARACTER)

HOW DO THE
CHARACTERS HANDLE
THE CHALLENGE?

ROUGH DRAFT
(CONSEQUENCES/ NEW PROBLEM)

WHAT CHOICES ARE THEY FORCED TO MAKE?

NEW SCENE

POV CHARACTER:

SCENE DESCRIPTIONS

USE FIVE SENSES - SIGHT, SMELL, SOUND, TASTE, TOUCH (TEXTURE)

ROUGH DRAFT
(GOAL OF SCENE)

WHAT IS THE MAIN CHARACTER THINKING AND FEELING DURING THIS SCENE?

ROUGH DRAFT
(PROBLEM OF THE SCENE)

WHAT ARE THE SIDE CHARACTERS THINKING AND FEELING?

ROUGH DRAFT

CHARACTERS TAKE ACTION - WHAT IS THE GOAL?

ROUGH DRAFT

HOW ARE THE CHARACTERS CHALLENGED?

ROUGH DRAFT
(CHOICES/ REVEALING CHARACTER)

HOW DO THE
CHARACTERS HANDLE
THE CHALLENGE?

ROUGH DRAFT
(CONSEQUENCES/ NEW PROBLEM)

WHAT CHOICES ARE THEY FORCED TO MAKE?

NEW SCENE

POV CHARACTER:

SCENE DESCRIPTIONS

USE FIVE SENSES - SIGHT, SMELL, SOUND, TASTE, TOUCH (TEXTURE)

ROUGH DRAFT
(GOAL OF SCENE)

WHAT IS THE MAIN CHARACTER THINKING AND FEELING DURING THIS SCENE?

ROUGH DRAFT
(PROBLEM OF THE SCENE)

WHAT ARE THE SIDE CHARACTERS THINKING AND FEELING?

ROUGH DRAFT

CHARACTERS TAKE ACTION - WHAT IS THE GOAL?

ROUGH DRAFT

HOW ARE THE CHARACTERS CHALLENGED?

ROUGH DRAFT
(CHOICES/ REVEALING CHARACTER)

HOW DO THE
CHARACTERS HANDLE
THE CHALLENGE?

ROUGH DRAFT
(CONSEQUENCES/ NEW PROBLEM)

WHAT CHOICES ARE THEY FORCED TO MAKE?

NEW SCENE

POV CHARACTER:

SCENE DESCRIPTIONS

USE FIVE SENSES - SIGHT, SMELL, SOUND, TASTE, TOUCH (TEXTURE)

ROUGH DRAFT
(GOAL OF SCENE)

WHAT IS THE MAIN CHARACTER THINKING AND FEELING DURING THIS SCENE?

ROUGH DRAFT
(PROBLEM OF THE SCENE)

WHAT ARE THE SIDE CHARACTERS THINKING AND FEELING?

ROUGH DRAFT

CHARACTERS TAKE ACTION - WHAT IS THE GOAL?

ROUGH DRAFT

HOW ARE THE CHARACTERS CHALLENGED?

ROUGH DRAFT
(CHOICES/ REVEALING CHARACTER)

HOW DO THE
CHARACTERS HANDLE
THE CHALLENGE?

ROUGH DRAFT (CONSEQUENCES/ NEW PROBLEM)	WHAT CHOICES ARE THEY FORCED TO MAKE?

NEW SCENE

POV CHARACTER:

SCENE DESCRIPTIONS

USE FIVE SENSES - SIGHT, SMELL, SOUND, TASTE, TOUCH (TEXTURE)

ROUGH DRAFT
(GOAL OF SCENE)

WHAT IS THE MAIN CHARACTER THINKING AND FEELING DURING THIS SCENE?

ROUGH DRAFT
(PROBLEM OF THE SCENE)

WHAT ARE THE SIDE CHARACTERS THINKING AND FEELING?

ROUGH DRAFT

CHARACTERS TAKE ACTION - WHAT IS THE GOAL?

ROUGH DRAFT

HOW ARE THE CHARACTERS CHALLENGED?

ROUGH DRAFT
(CHOICES/ REVEALING CHARACTER)

HOW DO THE
CHARACTERS HANDLE
THE CHALLENGE?

ROUGH DRAFT
(CONSEQUENCES/ NEW PROBLEM)

WHAT CHOICES ARE THEY FORCED TO MAKE?

NEW SCENE

POV CHARACTER:

SCENE DESCRIPTIONS

USE FIVE SENSES - SIGHT, SMELL, SOUND, TASTE, TOUCH (TEXTURE)

ROUGH DRAFT
(GOAL OF SCENE)

WHAT IS THE MAIN CHARACTER THINKING AND FEELING DURING THIS SCENE?

ROUGH DRAFT
(PROBLEM OF THE SCENE)

WHAT ARE THE SIDE CHARACTERS THINKING AND FEELING?

ROUGH DRAFT

CHARACTERS TAKE ACTION - WHAT IS THE GOAL?

ROUGH DRAFT

HOW ARE THE CHARACTERS CHALLENGED?

ROUGH DRAFT
(CHOICES/ REVEALING CHARACTER)

HOW DO THE
CHARACTERS HANDLE
THE CHALLENGE?

ROUGH DRAFT
(CONSEQUENCES/ NEW PROBLEM)

WHAT CHOICES ARE THEY FORCED TO MAKE?

NEW SCENE

POV CHARACTER:

SCENE DESCRIPTIONS

USE FIVE SENSES - SIGHT, SMELL, SOUND, TASTE, TOUCH (TEXTURE)

ROUGH DRAFT
(GOAL OF SCENE)

WHAT IS THE MAIN CHARACTER THINKING AND FEELING DURING THIS SCENE?

ROUGH DRAFT
(PROBLEM OF THE SCENE)

WHAT ARE THE SIDE CHARACTERS THINKING AND FEELING?

ROUGH DRAFT

CHARACTERS TAKE ACTION - WHAT IS THE GOAL?

ROUGH DRAFT

HOW ARE THE CHARACTERS CHALLENGED?

ROUGH DRAFT
(CHOICES/ REVEALING CHARACTER)

HOW DO THE
CHARACTERS HANDLE
THE CHALLENGE?

ROUGH DRAFT
(CONSEQUENCES/ NEW PROBLEM)

WHAT CHOICES ARE THEY FORCED TO MAKE?

NEW SCENE

POV CHARACTER:

SCENE DESCRIPTIONS

USE FIVE SENSES - SIGHT, SMELL, SOUND, TASTE, TOUCH (TEXTURE)

ROUGH DRAFT
(GOAL OF SCENE)

WHAT IS THE MAIN CHARACTER THINKING AND FEELING DURING THIS SCENE?

ROUGH DRAFT
(PROBLEM OF THE SCENE)

WHAT ARE THE SIDE CHARACTERS THINKING AND FEELING?

ROUGH DRAFT

CHARACTERS TAKE ACTION - WHAT IS THE GOAL?

ROUGH DRAFT

HOW ARE THE CHARACTERS CHALLENGED?

ROUGH DRAFT
(CHOICES/ REVEALING CHARACTER)

HOW DO THE CHARACTERS HANDLE THE CHALLENGE?

ROUGH DRAFT
(CONSEQUENCES/ NEW PROBLEM)

WHAT CHOICES ARE THEY FORCED TO MAKE?

NEW SCENE

POV CHARACTER:

SCENE DESCRIPTIONS

USE FIVE SENSES - SIGHT, SMELL, SOUND, TASTE, TOUCH (TEXTURE)

ROUGH DRAFT
(GOAL OF SCENE)

WHAT IS THE MAIN CHARACTER THINKING AND FEELING DURING THIS SCENE?

ROUGH DRAFT
(PROBLEM OF THE SCENE)

WHAT ARE THE SIDE CHARACTERS THINKING AND FEELING?

ROUGH DRAFT

CHARACTERS TAKE ACTION - WHAT IS THE GOAL?

ROUGH DRAFT

HOW ARE THE CHARACTERS CHALLENGED?

ROUGH DRAFT
(CHOICES/ REVEALING CHARACTER)

HOW DO THE
CHARACTERS HANDLE
THE CHALLENGE?

ROUGH DRAFT
(CONSEQUENCES/ NEW PROBLEM)

WHAT CHOICES ARE
THEY FORCED TO
MAKE?

NEW SCENE

POV CHARACTER:

SCENE DESCRIPTIONS

USE FIVE SENSES - SIGHT, SMELL, SOUND, TASTE, TOUCH (TEXTURE)

ROUGH DRAFT
(GOAL OF SCENE)

WHAT IS THE MAIN CHARACTER THINKING AND FEELING DURING THIS SCENE?

ROUGH DRAFT
(PROBLEM OF THE SCENE)

WHAT ARE THE SIDE CHARACTERS THINKING AND FEELING?

ROUGH DRAFT

CHARACTERS TAKE ACTION - WHAT IS THE GOAL?

ROUGH DRAFT

HOW ARE THE CHARACTERS CHALLENGED?

ROUGH DRAFT
(CHOICES/ REVEALING CHARACTER)

HOW DO THE CHARACTERS HANDLE THE CHALLENGE?

ROUGH DRAFT (CONSEQUENCES/ NEW PROBLEM)	WHAT CHOICES ARE THEY FORCED TO MAKE?

NEW SCENE

POV CHARACTER:

SCENE DESCRIPTIONS

USE FIVE SENSES - SIGHT, SMELL, SOUND, TASTE, TOUCH (TEXTURE)

ROUGH DRAFT
(GOAL OF SCENE)

WHAT IS THE MAIN CHARACTER THINKING AND FEELING DURING THIS SCENE?

ROUGH DRAFT
(PROBLEM OF THE SCENE)

WHAT ARE THE SIDE CHARACTERS THINKING AND FEELING?

ROUGH DRAFT

CHARACTERS TAKE ACTION - WHAT IS THE GOAL?

ROUGH DRAFT

HOW ARE THE CHARACTERS CHALLENGED?

ROUGH DRAFT
(CHOICES/ REVEALING CHARACTER)

HOW DO THE
CHARACTERS HANDLE
THE CHALLENGE?

ROUGH DRAFT
(CONSEQUENCES/ NEW PROBLEM)

WHAT CHOICES ARE THEY FORCED TO MAKE?

HE ANSWERED, “THE SCRIPTURES SAY:

BREAD ALONE WILL NOT SATISFY,
BUT TRUE LIFE IS FOUND IN EVERY WORD
THAT CONSTANTLY GOES FORTH FROM GOD’S MOUTH.”

MATT 4:4

ABOUT THE AUTHOR

JT HARRIS is a child of the Most High God, Author and Creator. The realms of Word, ink, and song are where she loves to explore, have many adventures, and sometimes take rest. She is a homeschooling mother of two children, a wife of a loving husband, and has a family dog named Ben.

"...Let everything you say be good and helpful, so that your words will be an encouragement to those who hear them."
- Eph 4:29

For more writer resources, journals, and family fiction head to:

www.jtharris.ca

Made in United States
North Haven, CT
23 January 2026

86821441R00120